the john ritchie

family series

let's talk about GIVING

JOHN RITCHIE LTD
CHRISTIAN PUBLICATIONS

Typeset & Print: Campsie Litho, 51 French Street, Glasgow. 0141-554 5225

Graphic Design: Graeme Hewitson

Illustrations: J. Glen

Contents

Should I give?

On accepting the Lord Jesus Christ as your Saviour, one of the first things which you come to know is that God is love. As a result of this you soon appreciate that love must find a way of expressing itself. You come to understand that there is a link between loving and giving. God is a giving God. Loving and giving are inextricably linked in the Scriptures. "The Son of God, who loved me, and gave Himself for me" (Gal 2:20), and "God so loved the world that He gave His only begotten son" (John 3:16), are only two of the verses which emphasise this truth.

There is a link between loving and giving

Right at the beginning of the Bible, the very first recorded act in the lives of the two men who were born first into the world, is that they give to God. Abel gives what is acceptable to God, and Cain gives what is not acceptable, but nevertheless they both had a desire to give. As you have received blessings far greater than those which were enjoyed by Cain or Abel you surely, in turn, must want to express the love which you have for the Lord Jesus by giving to Him.

In the Old Testament, Israelites were instructed to give a tithe, or ten percent, of their income to the Lord. Is this is what we have to give as believers? If this is so, there is a simple arithmetic calculation to be done, and then we can be satisfied that we have pleased God by giving what He asks, without any great care or consideration on our part. You may, on the other hand, consider that such a method of giving was part of the Law, and as you are not under the Law today, you do not need to give one tenth of your income, confident that the Lord will be satisfied with much less.

With this in mind you wonder what is the correct course of action when you cannot afford to give away one tenth of your income. Do you still give and suffer loss and sacrifice, or do you limit the amount which you give until perhaps you are giving little or nothing?

This can be a particular problem in a family when children are small and resources are severely limited.

Another issue is whether giving is limited to your finances or includes anything else which you possess. Does the Lord look for more than a percentage of your regular income, and if so, what does He seek and how do you give it?

In family life you may feel it necessary to ensure that all the needs of the children are met before you give anything, because the money given into your charge is for that purpose primarily and only the excess is for distribution to others. How can you give if your own needs are not met?

Having then considered these issues and decided how much you wish to give, you must determine when and how. There are many different ways of giving, and a great number of people and causes seem to be worthy of support. How can you possibly decide which of these will be the recipients of your gifts?

You will need to address all these issues as you consider this important subject in the life of a believer. The subject of giving is one which you may avoid because you would rather not face up to its demands. You may wish to keep all the resources which are given to you and hoard them for your own use and for your own pleasure. If you think like this, be thankful that God did not act in such a manner. If He had, the Lord Jesus would never have been given to die on the cross, and you would never have known salvation. You have eternal life because God gave. How will you respond to being a recipient of such liberal, unselfish bounty?

How will you respond?

Should I tithe?

The first question is whether you should tithe your income. Are you expected to give one tenth of your income to the work of the Lord? Let us look at what tithing involved.

Instructions for tithing

"Thou shalt truly tithe all the increase of thy field"(Deut 14:22).

"Behold I have given the children of Levi all the tenth in Israel for an inheritance, for their service which they serve"(Num 18:21).

The Israelite was instructed to give one tenth of his income to the Lord for the maintenance of the Levites in their service in the Tabernacle. The Levites possessed no lands and were not able to grow their own food, nor provide for their families through buying and selling. One tenth of the harvest, and the firstborn of the flock, was to be set aside to be given to the Levites. If people lived too far from Jerusalem to bring these offerings they were to turn them into money and bring this to Jerusalem to purchase there what they would offer. Tithing was to be carried out year by year as a constant reminder of how much they owed to the Lord who had redeemed them out of Egypt's slavery.

The question of whether they could afford the tithe is not mentioned. Rather, the opposite view is stated, that the giving of the tithe enabled the Lord their God to bless them in all the work which they did (Deut 14:29). The benefit, not the cost, is emphasised.

Other offerings

As you study the requirements of the Law, however, you see that more was expected of the godly Israelite than simply the giving of the tithe. The tithe, which was obligatory, was to be supplemented with a series of offerings which were voluntary.

The Israelite who truly wished to show his appreciation to the Lord would bring his offering to the Lord. This could consist of a burnt offering, a meal offering, or a peace offering (Lev 1,2,3). These were all voluntary and the offerer would reveal the depth of his appreciation to, and love for the Lord in the nature of the offering which he brought. This offering would need to be taken from the flocks which he possessed, or purchased with money which he could have used for other purposes. The desire to give, however, was so great, that he was prepared to sacrifice his own needs, to give to God what would please Him. The sin offering or the trespass offering was also to be brought when sin or trespass had been committed, again using the resources which the Lord had given the offerer. It is not our purpose here to deal with the significance of these offerings, but simply to show that the Israelite who loved the Lord would be prepared to sacrifice in order to give to the Lord.

Sacrifice in order to give to the Lord

Additional provision is made in Leviticus 27 for those who vow to give to the Lord further tokens of appreciation for His goodness. A man or woman could be devoted to the Lord. An animal, a house or a field could all similarly be vowed or devoted. These were to be valued by the priest and the equivalent money value was to be given to the Lord. This was normally stored in the temple and used for the service which was carried out in these hallowed courts. Instructions on how this valuation was to be made are clearly set down. If, for instance, a man wished to show his complete devotion to the Lord he would go to the priest and have himself valued. If the person was between five and twenty years of age, the value was twenty shekels for a male and ten for a female. If it was a child under five years of age the value was five shekels for a male and three shekels for a female. The corresponding value for those aged twenty to sixty years of age was fifty and thirty shekels. Thus, once again, devotion was expressed by giving.

In addition to the valuation of persons there were instructions given for the valuation of possessions. Animals, houses and fields could all be given to the Lord. There was no limit to the expressions of gratitude and appreciation which the Israelite could offer.

Even all this does not exhaust the opportunities which were available for those who loved the Lord to show the depth of their feelings. It emphasises that although the tithe was an obligation, it was expected however, that devoted souls would wish to do much more than simply meet their minimum obligation.

What should I give?

All you possess is His

"Know ye not . . . ye are not your own? For ye are bought with a price" (1 Cor 6:20).

It is vital to understand that money is not the only thing that has to be given to the Lord. The price paid for us at Calvary has given Him the right to possess us completely. As a believer, all that you have belongs to the Lord. Nothing is your possession exclusively, and therefore your resources must not be in separate compartments, one containing what is yours and another what belongs to Him. This broadens greatly your ideas about giving. It is valuable to see now what some believers did give to the service of the Lord.

All that you have belongs to the Lord

You will find in 2 Corinthians 8:5 an important statement about those who gave of their money for the purpose of relieving the need of the poor believers in Judaea : "They first gave their own selves to the Lord, and unto us by the will of God". Giving yourself is the starting point. Do not miss this first important step. Give yourself, and then your values will be adjusted to the values of heaven, allowing you to see clearly how your possessions should be used.

A good example of what can be given to the Lord is found in the lives of Aquila and Priscilla. This godly husband and wife were active in the service of the Lord Jesus when Paul was preaching the gospel. Look at what is written in the Scriptures regarding this couple.

Giving yourself is the starting point

o They gave their home

"He (Paul) abode with them" (Acts 18:3).

Aquila was a Jew who, together with his wife Priscilla was forced to leave Rome because Claudius had commanded all Jews to leave that city. They made their home in the city of Corinth, and when Paul arrived there to preach the gospel they opened their home to him. This godly couple could have argued that they had suffered too much upset in their home life to take in a stranger, but they had such a desire to serve the Lord that they were willing to provide hospitality for the apostle. Like Paul, they were tentmakers, and this gave them a shared interest, but it was the gospel which really linked them together.

In Romans 16:5 you meet Aquila and Priscilla once more, this time back in Rome. Paul greets them, together with the church which was in their house. They extended hospitality to believers wherever they were living. Indeed in 1 Corinthians 16:19 they are found in Ephesus and are still opening their home to the believers. You can truly say of Aquila and Priscilla that they gave their home to the Lord, no matter where they were living. And in this they were not alone. The church in Colosse enjoyed hospitality in the home of Philemon (Philemon 2). Philip the evangelist provided accommodation for Paul on his journey to Jerusalem (Acts 21:8).

It is good for a young couple to determine that they will be known as willing hosts to other believers. The benefit which they receive from fellowship in their home will far outweigh the costs involved. Do not imagine that the purpose of hospitality is to provide the most lavish or expensive meal possible. Simple fare will be sufficient and will be much appreciated by those you receive. Many a lonely, tired, troubled believer has been helped by simple hospitality in the homes of those who were prepared to use just what they had for the work of the Lord. Many young believers without christian homes have spent happy hours in the homes of those who have a care for their spiritual well-being.

If you give to the Lord in this way you will find your life to be immeasurably enriched. Conversations round the table, impressions made on you by godly men and women, and the gratitude of those whom you helped, will all add lustre to your life and service. This is part of your work in the local church.

The pressures of modern society have resulted in this work being carried out less than in years gone past. Some believers find that their time at home is so restricted that they wish to keep the precious hours with their family free from the intrusion of others. Even on Lord's Day the work of preparing for guests, and the effort which is necessary to make their visit pleasant and profitable, is looked on with dismay and avoided. Peace and quiet is all that you may wish in your home, but is this using for the Lord what He has given you?

The exhortation of Hebrews 13:1 is an encouragement: "Be not forgetful to entertain strangers: for thereby some have entertained angels unawares". Hospitality towards those whom you know is commendable, but do not leave it there. Extend a welcome to other believers who may come into your area as strangers. And who might you welcome into your home? Some, without knowing it, entertained angels! Perhaps you will not do that, but the results of this work may well be far beyond your expectations.

You will find your life immeasurably enriched

o They gave their time

"They took him unto them, and expounded unto him the way of God more perfectly" (Acts 18:26).

You have seen already that the home life of Aquila and Priscilla in Rome was interrupted by the decree of the Emperor. Subsequently they seem to have moved house on a number of occasions. Despite this they were prepared to give of their time in the service of the Master. When Apollos came to Ephesus, where Aquila and Priscilla then lived, it was clear that although he was enthusiastic in the Lord's service and mighty in the Scriptures, he required further teaching.

Aquila and Priscilla gave of their time to undertake this task. This would involve not only opening their home to him, but spending long hours over the Scriptures debating the issues and instructing this mighty man. They could have argued that their paths might never cross again and that they personally would gain little benefit from Apollos in years to come. But they did not look on this task like that. There was work to be done for the Master and they were able to do it, so they gave themselves and their time to it.

We live in a busy world where so little of our time seems to be available for the work of the Lord. Pressure from work and all the other things which crowd in seem to use up all of the 'free' time which we have, leaving very little for the study of the Scriptures and for the work of the Lord. It is good practice to determine to use your time wisely and give it to Him. There are regular meetings of the local church which must not be neglected. This does not, however, fulfil all your obligations. In any locality there are those who are ill and who need to be visited. There are those who find themselves in trouble and distress and who, consequently, need support; those who are lonely and who need to be encouraged. If you look about you there are many ways in which your time can be usefully employed, but you must firstly determine to give it to Him.

If you think only of yourself you will find plenty to fill your days and occupy your hours. There is no shortage of activities which are legitimate and involve nothing sinful. The question which you must ask, however, is - what benefit is there to the Lord's work in these pursuits? Times of relaxation and rest are necessary, but you cannot use all your free time for this and feel that you have given to the Lord Jesus all that is possible.

Use your time wisely and give it to Him

12

This does not give you licence to ignore necessary family duties and responsibilities. The diligent servant of the Lord will ensure that what has to be done is done, but having carried out all necessary duties, the Lord will be given what time is available.

○ They gave their neck

"Who have for my life laid down their own necks" (Rom 16:4).

Priscilla and Aquila would stop at nothing in their desire to help the spread of the gospel. All the churches of the Gentiles owed them thanks for their selfless service. They were united in it. They had "laid down their own necks". They had decided before the Lord that their home, their time, their possessions and even their own necks would be devoted to Him. There was no half-hearted devotion here! They were united in their desire to give all, and were prepared to go as far as giving even their lives in His service. Is this not the ultimate in giving? So devoted were they that they would have faced martyrdom to further the work of the Lord.

No half-hearted devotion!

How should I give?

Having seen that love for the Lord Jesus Christ will produce in us a desire to give Him everything, let us now consider how we give financially.

As the believers in Corinth gathered to hear the reading of the first letter which had been sent to them by the apostle Paul, there must have been a mixture of feelings in their hearts. In chapters 1 - 6, there had been corrective teaching which would leave them feeling chastened, with a determination to put matters right. But as chapter 15 was read their spirits would soar. Not only was this the answer to those who were troubling them by teaching that there was no resurrection of the dead, but the very grandeur of what was read would lift their spirits. This surely was Paul's way of closing his letter on a high note, leaving them rejoicing in the greatness of their God and the salvation which they enjoyed.

A desire to give, in order to help others

But as they prepared to leave, the scribe read on. Paul was not finished. What else did he have to say which could lift them even higher? As they listen they hear these words: "Now concerning the collection for the saints . . ." Paul had brought them right back down to earth again! He was not finished until he had shown the practical effects which such teaching should have on them. One of the effects was that their pockets would be touched as well as their hearts, and that they would have a desire to give, in order to help others. The poor believers in Jerusalem required financial assistance, and other believers should be affected by their circumstances and be ready to give to meet the need. The apostle takes this opportunity to tell them how to give, and the exhortation regarding this collection for the saints teaches us the New Testament principles of giving.

Give regularly

"Upon the first day of the week let every one of you lay by him in store" (1 Cor 16:2).

The believers came together on the first day of the week and this was a suitable time to give. As you remember the Lord Jesus in the breaking of bread, your consideration of Him will encourage you to give to Him. Paul did not want there to be an unseemly rush to gather up monies when he came to visit, rather that there should be orderly gatherings of money each week, and when he arrived it would be ready to take to Jerusalem. In encouraging them to act in this way he is encouraging us also to consider our giving on the first day of every week.

The gathering to which Paul referred was made at home, as each family set aside the amount which they had decided to give to the relief fund. Today it is the custom to take what you decide to give and to place it in a box or a bag made available for that purpose each Lord's Day morning. This is possible today with the banking facilities which can be used, but obviously there must be a determination of the amount at home before you come.

Consider, weekly at least, how much you will give

It is, therefore, good practice to consider, weekly at least, how much you will give. Even if you are paid on a monthly basis, it is still good practice to consider your giving at regular intervals and give, because circumstances change from time to time. It is so easy to fall into the habit of very mechanical giving with no consideration of how much or to whom the money should be given.

Perhaps having faced up to the challenge of giving you pull back and decide to leave things as they are. You fear that if you did examine the position closely you would find that you should be giving more, and that you could be giving more. This would affect the amount of money in your pocket, and you prefer not to raise the question!

Heed the exhortation given to the Corinthians. Be constantly considering how you can give, and regularly "lay by in store" of your money for the furtherance of the work of the Lord.

Give after personal consideration

"Every man according as he purposeth in his heart" (2 Cor 9:7).

Each household has to tackle this issue independently. No one has authority to impose on others the amount which they must give. The need to give a stated amount which is pressed upon you by others is not the scriptural way.

The practice of the early church in Jerusalem to pool their resources and have all things common was a result of persecution and the difficult days through which they were passing (Acts 2:44). In Corinth Paul did not teach that such a method was to be used for handling money and other assets.

This did not mean that what they possessed belonged to them exclusively. You have already seen that all you have belongs to the Lord. Giving is to be an individual exercise before the Lord, and thus it was that each one had to lay by in store. There was to be no 'league table' of donations. There is to be no list by which others would become aware of what you had given, or you become aware of what they had given. This is a matter between the individual and the Lord. Public lists of how much is given, or any means by which such details become known, are not scriptural.

Such information made public would be damaging and dangerous. Those who gave most might be given a position which they should not have, and those who gave less could be treated as of less value. Yet in the arithmetic of heaven the latter may be greater than the former. The words of the Lord Jesus regarding the giving of alms, "let not thy right hand know what they left hand doeth" (Matt

6:3), is enough to confirm to us that absolute secrecy should surround your giving.

Secrecy should surround your giving

Every one is expected to give

"Let every one of you lay by in store" (1 Cor 16:2).

It is expected that every believer will have a desire to give to the Lord. You must not look around your local church and feel that there are enough people with more wealth than you, and therefore there is no need for you to give. To act like this shows a basic misunderstanding of Bible teaching. You have an opportunity to give and have fellowship in meeting a need or furthering a work for God. If you fail to respond you will have missed an opportunity which may never come your way again. The question is not, 'Can someone else meet that need' but is rather 'Can I have fellowship in this?' By responding positively, you lay up treasure in heaven which would not have been there if you had failed to give.

It is true that there are times when resources will be stretched, and you will not be able to give as much as you would like to. Do not, however, use this as an excuse for giving nothing. As you consider the question of how much you should give, you will see that the arithmetic of heaven differs from the arithmetic of earth. You must never consider that your giving is too little to be of any consequence, and therefore it can be overlooked.

So neither the wealth of others nor the small amounts that you can spare are barriers to giving. But when resources are adequate or abundant it is still possible for you to neglect giving. It is a strange feature of human nature that the more you possess the more reluctant you can be to give! No matter what the cause, however, a lack of exercise in giving is an indication that a person is not in a healthy spiritual state.

Lay up treasure in heaven

It has to be willing

"Not grudgingly or of necessity: for God loveth a cheerful giver" (2 Cor 9:7).

Even those who give, can do so with the wrong attitude. It is possible to look with great regret at what you have determined to give. You think of what you could have purchased with this money, of the extra comforts which you could have enjoyed or of the extra holidays it could have helped to provide. Although you give with a smile on your face, there is no smile in your heart. You are not a cheerful giver, you are a resentful giver, feeling that the Lord is demanding too much from you, maybe even taking what is yours to use as you think fit. You are giving only because your husband or wife considers it necessary and you do not share their views. You may even be giving because there is a need for money in the local church and the expense has to be cleared somehow, so you give what you have to more out of duty than with enthusiasm.

Do you fall into any of these categories of which Paul writes here? The first is the grudging giver who wishes to retain what he has given. The second gives out of necessity because he is under compulsion to do so. In both of these cases the giver will look sorrowfully at what he has gifted and regard it as a loss which he would rather not have sustained.

How much better to be the cheerful giver whom God loves. This cheerful giver feels no sense of loss or sorrow at what has been given, does not regard the gift as wasted resources, but as that which is given to the Lord as an expression of devotion. Love, he understands, is always expressed by giving. As far as the question of losing is concerned you will see in a later section that giving to God involves no loss whatsoever.

Financial giving -
How much do I give?

The question of how much you should give to the Lord is one which often causes deep heart-searching. As we have seen, there is no arithmetical formula given in Scripture. You are left to decide for yourself what should be laid by for the work of the Lord.

You may feel that a simple formula would solve this problem, without causing you any heart-searching. This is exactly why a formula would not do! Such a method of giving would be a demand which God placed upon you. It would be almost a bill which had to be paid every week or month and would be regarded as payment for the goodness of God in your life. I am sure you can see the dangers which would attend such an approach to giving.

Love is not expressed by the payment of a bill. Love is expressed by a voluntary act of giving. God is pleased when you take time to consider carefully what you wish to give, and then give it gladly, not out of a sense of paying a bill, but of loving willingness.

**Give as God has
prospered you**

Calculating how much

"As God hath prospered" (1 Cor 16:2).

The advice which was given to the Corinthians still holds good today. You give as God has prospered you. You give what you can afford to give. Thus there is not being placed on your shoulders an intolerable burden which you cannot bear. If giving does show your love to another, the recipient of the gift also shows love by not expecting you to place on yourself a burden which you cannot bear.

This does mean that there will be great exercise of heart before the Lord to decide how much. Husband and wife should be in agreement in this vital matter so that one of them does not feel that too much or even too little is being given. The needs of wife and family have to be taken into account. It would not be honouring to the Lord to give so much, that they were neglected and seen to be in want.

There is one fundamental point which we must get right or else our giving will not be as it should. Paul tells us that there must first be a willing mind (2 Cor 8:12). Approach the subject with a mind prepared to give, not with the attitude that this is an imposition laid upon you.

The family budget

It is good practice to have discipline in the family budget. Each family must, before the Lord, determine its priorities. There are a number of guide-lines which apply.

Those who are newly married are under great pressure today to stretch themselves to the financial limits in purchasing and furnishing their new home. It is commendable that a new husband wishes to give his wife the best that can be obtained, but care must be taken that the financial pressures under which you place yourselves are not so great that they add extra strain to your marriage and take away any opportunity you have to give to the Lord. It is good to put Him first in these first important purchases of your married life.

Disposable and non-disposable income

A large part of your income will be taken up with the necessary expenses of living. As your income increases you can increase your standard of living accordingly and use the extra resources to enable you to move to a larger house, to own larger cars, to enjoy more expensive holidays, if you so wish.

Often such increases in expenditure are necessary. A larger

house may be needed for a growing family. A holiday can be of spiritual as well as physical benefit. It is possible, however, to become unwise in the use of all that the Lord has given

you. There are pressures around us today to be seen to possess what the world regards as the outward trappings of success. You must be careful that you are not becoming carried away with this spirit of the age which will result in you becoming a slave to materialism.

When material prosperity comes your way, you must consider firstly how you will use what you have for the work of the Lord, and not merely take into account your wants. The prosperity which you enjoy is not of your own making. It is, as Paul reminds us, God who has prospered us. Do ensure that, as you have increased resources, you do not spend them in self-gratification, but give more to His service.

As you have increased resources, give more to His service

When resources are small

"In a great trial of affliction . . . their deep poverty abounded unto the riches of their liberality" (2 Cor 8:2).

Many believers go though times when funds become very limited. In such circumstances there is always the temptation to discontinue giving until the position improves. However, even in these straits those who love the Lord will seek to give something, no matter how small.

In the city of Jerusalem there was a poor widow who desired to give to God. She looked at what she possessed and it totalled two mites. This was worth almost nothing, and she must have felt a sense of despair when she considered all that she had at her disposal. She could have reasoned that there was no point in going to the temple to put so little into the treasury. The many rich men who frequented the temple courts would give sums which to her were beyond comprehension. In one day they would give more than she could hope to possess in a lifetime. She could also have reasoned that little though it was, the two mites were necessary to buy some food. Surely, when her total wealth amounted to two mites, God would not expect anything from her. As she weighed up these issues little did she realise that heaven was interested in the choice which she would make. Her decision was to give, not one of the mites, but both of them, so she proceeded to the temple to cast them in among the valuable coins which were being deposited there. Thus she would show her devotion to the God whom she loved. But would He notice such a paltry gift?

Heaven was interested in the choice

As she approached the treasury the Lord Jesus was watching. The well-dressed, prominent members of society were casting their gifts in, openly and ostentatiously. She approaches and quickly throws in the two mites. Did she realise that He was observing her every move? How much, then, is two mites worth? Greater in value than anything received that day, declares the Lord! How could this possibly be?

The exchange rate of heaven

"This poor widow hath cast more in, than all they which have cast into the treasury" (Mark 12:43).

How vital it is to understand that the Lord did not value her gift according to the currencies of earth but according to the currency of heaven. As for any currency it is necessary to apply an exchange rate to determine its value in another currency, so you must apply the heavenly exchange rate to assess the value of these two mites in the currency of heaven. How then do you arrive at the exchange rate? The Lord Jesus uses the rate based on the devotion of your heart. Thus what is little on earth when multiplied by this exchange rate can become worth very much. This poor widow showed her devotion by giving all that she had. So, her little became much and was highly valued in heaven. But you must also remember that where there is no devotion of heart, large amounts given will be multiplied by an exchange rate which reduces their value considerably. It is even possible for devotion to be so low that in the currency of heaven the value is converted to zero.

Paul further emphasises this point in 2 Corinthians 8:12. The amount which individual Corinthians gave for the relief of the poor in Judaea would not be measured by the Lord on the basis of its worth in the currencies of earth. There had first to be a willing mind, and then what the giver had left, as well as what he had given would be taken into account. If this was not so the rich would have an advantage over the poor which could not be reversed.

In the account of the widow casting in her two mites to the temple treasury, the whole point which the Lord Jesus is emphasising is that motive is all important as you consider how much you will give. Do not measure your giving against the scale of the need which you are seeking to meet, and decide that your little is too insignificant to count. Do not think that large sums given are automatically pleasing to God. The poor widow gave to the limit of her ability. How do you measure up to an example like that? What is the heavenly exchange rate in your life? Does it increase or decrease the value of your giving?

How much?

"Not that other men be eased, and ye burdened" (2 Cor 8:13).

As you decide, one further factor must be taken into account. You are not giving so that others may live in luxury and at ease, while you bear the financial burden of supporting them. Anyone living is such ease and luxury would

not be a suitable recipient of believers' gifts. By giving to those in need, or by supporting those who require finance from others because they are giving their time and energies to the work of the Lord, you are creating an equality, so that the resources given by the Lord to His people are evenly distributed. Remember also Paul's warning of the possibility of you some day being in want, and finding that others will need to share their resources with you (2 Cor 8:14).

The Lord is looking on as you give

The decision is therefore left to you. As you make it, do not feed self-gratification first. Meet your obligations, but do not burden yourself with over-ambition in material things. Remember that heaven is watching your decision-making process and the Lord is looking on as you give. What value will He place on the gift which you decide to offer to Him?

To whom should I give?

After deciding how much you will give, you are faced with the decision of who should receive from you. You must not deal with this in a slipshod way, without due care and attention. Resources have to be put to the best and most worthy use, and it is wise to consider all the issues in a prayerful manner.

Consider all the issues in a prayerful manner

Giving through the local church

"No church communicated with me concerning giving and receiving, but ye only" (Phil 4:15).

The local church will be one of your main channels of giving. In the early part of the Acts of the Apostles, the Christians had all things common. In this way they regarded their possessions as belonging to all the believers. In Acts 6 where you read the story of Ananias and Sapphira it is clear that all possessions were not pooled, although some did sell what they owned and gave it to the apostles. Barnabas did this and Ananias and Sapphira tried to imitate them, with tragic results. When Paul wrote to the Corinthians, as you have seen, the believers gave weekly.

Now, in the local church, each Lord's Day an offering will be uplifted and you will give as the Lord has prospered you. Generally this offering has a three-fold purpose.

Some of the money gathered will be used to meet the cost of upkeep of the buildings in which the believers meet and to finance the activities which are carried on there. Remember that in these matters you are paying your own legitimate expenses and are not giving to others. It is essential, however, that buildings are well maintained and not left to become dilapidated and shoddy. These buildings are only bricks and mortar. They are not 'sanctified' nor are they a 'sanctuary', but to use buildings which are run down is not a good testimony in the neighbourhood.

Every area of the work of the Lord in which you engage must also be adequately funded. Your literature must be of good quality; your Sunday School prizes must not be the cheapest obtainable. There must never be a seedy, cheap feel about any of the Lord's work. Thus you will give to ensure that you not need be ashamed of any aspect of the Lord's work for which you are responsible.

The second use of these offerings is the support of the work of the Lord in other areas. It is good practice to maintain an interest in those who are working at home and overseas in the Lord's service. The elders who discuss these matters will be pleased to listen to any suggestion you have to make as to how these funds should be distributed. It is beneficial to keep a keen interest in work which is being carried on in other areas. Do not become too parochial in your outlook.

Keep a keen interest in work in other areas

The third use of the offerings will be to help those who are in need of financial or material support. On more than one occasion Paul exhorted his readers to give for the poor saints who were in Judaea. By doing this you will show your love and fellowship in the Lord Jesus and will assist them, not only materially, but spiritually. One common practice today is to gather together goods and supplies which are forwarded to missionaries abroad, to meet their own needs and the needs of those among whom they labour. This is an excellent method of giving, but remember only to send what you would use yourself. Second hand goods may still be useful, but do not insult people by sending what is worn out, old fashioned and fit only for the rubbish bin!

Private giving

"He oft refreshed me" (2 Tim 1:16).

In addition to giving through the local church you may decide to give privately. Would Aquila and Priscilla not have assisted the apostle Paul financially? Onesiphorus is mentioned in 2 Timothy 1:16

as one who had "oft refreshed" the apostle Paul when he was imprisoned. Could this not include providing clothing and some other comforts which would have made conditions more bearable? No great details are given in the New Testament of this form of giving as it would be carried out quietly and privately. "Let us do good unto all men, especially unto them who are of the household of faith" (Gal 6:10), however, encourages us to give privately wherever there is need which we can help to meet.

Give privately wherever there is need

Situations may come to your attention which require immediate support and which cannot wait for the local church organising a special offering for this specific purpose. There are areas of the Lord's work in which you have a personal interest which may not be shared by others. There will be work which you wish to support which you feel you cannot ask the local church to share as it is not well known to them.

This area of giving does not replace the regular giving on a Lord's Day but is in addition to it. The danger which it raises is that an individual gives with the feeling that the gift gives some right of control over the recipient. Those who give large sums may feel that those to whom they give are under some sort of obligation to them. It should be remembered that once money is set aside for the work of the Lord you cease to have control over it. The recipient of your gift is receiving what you have given to the Lord, and therefore is accepting it as from the Lord. Obviously there will be gratitude for what you have given, but there is no obligation to you as a result of the gift. The obligation of the recipient is to the Lord, to use it for His glory.

A further danger of private giving is that you may feel tempted to reveal to others details of gifts which you have distributed. You may

Keep your actions completely confidential

wish to gain some respect or reputation by acting in this way, but by so doing you are seeking your reward now rather than leaving it until you appear at the Judgement Seat of Christ. Keep your actions in this area completely confidential.

The cycle of giving

Perhaps you are feeling at this stage that this subject is fine for a booklet or for teaching from the platform or pulpit, but you doubt whether it is really practical in the pressing economic circumstances of the present day. Was it acceptable in the calmer society in which the Bible was written, and will it really work in the days of stress and pressure in which most believers find themselves?

Will it really work?

You do believe that the truth of the Scriptures is not limited to one particular era of history, but applies to every age. As a believer you cannot retreat from that position. Should you do so, you are denying that this is the Word of God which "liveth and abideth for ever". These principles of giving, therefore, apply currently, no matter what economic stringencies you face.

It is helpful when you consider these issues to understand the cycle of giving which is found in 2 Corinthians 9. The Corinthians were being asked to give for the relief of the poor and their giving would be helped if they clearly understood how God ordered the cycle of giving. Paul lays this out for us in 2 Corinthians 9:10.

God gives the seed

"He that ministereth seed to the sower . . ."

The picture which Paul takes up is that of a sower scattering his seed. The first step in the cycle of giving is to realise that God gives us the seed. It is God who has given you the resources which you have. The sower obtaining seed, has two options available to him. He can retain the seed for his own use and decide that it will

all be consumed in this manner. If that it is his decision he will have no seed to sow. Initially he may not be aware of the implications of this, because he will appear to have more than the sower who is using only some of his seed to meet his own needs and is sowing the remainder in his fields. Initially, therefore, it appears that the sower who decides to retain all his seed for his own consumption and for the use of his family, appears to have far greater resources than the sower who uses as much as possible to sow.

The sower receives bread

"both minister bread for your food . . ."

Here you are beginning to see the wisdom of the man who has been sowing. Those who have consumed everything for their own use will have no harvest and, as a result, no further bread or seed. The sower, however, finds that the God who gave him the seed to sow has now met his need by providing bread from the fruits of the harvest. The point at issue here is that God cares for the sower and meets his need. Those who sow their resources in the service of the Lord will find that He does provide for all the needs of their lives, just as surely as harvest follows sowing.

God cares for the sower and meets his need

It is of interest to note that the Philippians had forwarded gifts to the apostle Paul on more than one occasion (Phil 4:16). On that basis Paul can declare to them with confidence that just as they had provided for his need, so the Lord will provide for their need (Phil 4:18-19). There is no promise that you will receive all that you want, but you can be assured that you will receive what is necessary to meet the requirements of life.

The sower receives surplus

"and multiply your seed sown . . ."

But bread to satisfy need is not all that the sower receives at

harvest time. God provides him with a
surplus so that he now has a
further supply of seed to sow.
The purpose of this is to
ensure that the cycle of the
harvest can be continued, and
similarly, it is His wish that the cycle
of giving should be continued. There is
little need to impress on you that the greater
the quantity of seed which you sow, the greater will be the harvest.
Just as the harvest is in a yearly cycle so the Lord provides for you to
give and to keep on giving.

The cycle starts again

"and increase the fruits of righteousness."

It must not be thought that this is a guarantee from the Lord
that the generous giver will become financially wealthy. There is no
promise in the Bible that faithfulness to the Lord is rewarded with an
increase in your worldly wealth. To consider this to be so, and to wish for
it to be so, is to fall into the trap of which Paul warns in 1 Timothy 6:9–
10: "They that will be rich fall into temptation and a snare".

The fruits of righteousness which are increased are the evidence
of your christian growth. The reward which you seek is not material,
that which will pass away. You want something far more permanent
than that!

And so you have learned the consistency of God's dealings. As
with the sower and the harvest, so He will deal with us, multiplying
your seed as you scatter it and giving enough in return to satisfy
your needs and enable us to keep up the work of sowing.

**The consistency
of God's dealings**

Paul sums this up in 2 Corinthians 9:8, "and God is able to
make all grace abound toward you; that ye, always having all
sufficiency in all things, may abound to every good work".

Who are the beneficiaries of giving?

You may feel that this is a rather obvious question to ask which requires no answer. Surely the beneficiaries of giving are those who receive! While that is undoubtedly true it is worth looking again at 2 Corinthians 9:6-15 to see if there are any other beneficiaries.

The giver receives

Does this surprise you? In the cycle of giving which we have just considered, one beneficiary is the sower, because he has bread given to him. This is what is mentioned first. Thus those who give, do benefit from their act as God takes account of their liberality and ensures that their resources will continue to be sufficient.

The truly compassionate heart will act by giving

The recipient receives

This service supplies the wants of the saints, so they feel the benefit of the generous giving of other believers. Just speaking about compassion for others will incur no great cost, but the truly compassionate heart will open up towards the needs of others and act by giving to relieve need, distress, poverty and disease. What may be little to you may mean a great deal to the recipient.

God receives

Paul emphasises this in three verses: "Bountifulness...which causeth through us thanksgiving to God" (2 Cor 9:11); "Abundant also by many thanksgivings unto God" (2 Cor 9:12); and "Whiles by the experiment of this ministration they glorify God ......for your liberal distribution unto them, and unto all men" (2 Cor 9:13). So thanksgiving to God was rising from the heart of Paul and from the hearts of those who were benefiting from the gift. They were conscious of the fact that although thanks were due to those who had given of their substance, the prime object of their gratitude was God who had moved the hearts of others and provided the resources to make the giving possible.

The prime object of their gratitude was God

Encouragements to give

It may be that, as you read these pages, you are still questioning whether you will be able to follow the scriptural teaching on giving, thinking that its demands are too onerous. You may well consider it a good practice, but realistically you do not feel that you will be able to keep up the momentum and give constantly and consistently as you ought. If you are honest enough to admit that to yourself do not be dismayed, because many before you have had the same doubts and fears. In order to help you, Scripture does point out some examples of others who have given in a way which was pleasing to God.

The example of other believers

"The grace of God bestowed on the churches of Macedonia" (2 Cor 8:1).

The churches of Macedonia had given liberally for the relief of the poor believers who were in Judaea. In view of this you must not be tempted to think that their circumstances were so favourable that they had more than enough to meet all their need, with plenty left over for distribution to others. Neither must you consider that they lived a pleasant life of ease which made giving a very easy thing to do. The truth is very different.

These Macedonian believers were enduring times of great affliction and persecution. Life was not easy, and to the onlooker it would appear that they were more needing to receive than to give. In addition to the persecution they were suffering, they were living in deep poverty, with few resources apparently available to meet their own needs, before any thought could be given to the needs of others.

When they gave, however, they gave beyond their power. They gave beyond their ability and far beyond the expectations which Paul had for them.

If they could give, how much more can you?

Thus the example of these poor Christians speaks to us over the centuries. If they could give, how much more can you? If they did so out of poverty and in circumstances of persecution and affliction, how much more can you as you enjoy the material prosperity of this age?

It is worth noting in v.13 that the giving of the Corinthians is evidence of the proof of the reality of their profession. Their "professed subjection" to the gospel of Christ was seen to be real by their willingness to give.

The example of the Lord Jesus

"Ye know the grace of our Lord Jesus Christ, that, though He was rich, yet for your sakes He became poor, that ye through His poverty might be rich" (2 Cor 8:9).

This is the greatest example of giving which has ever been seen. Writing to the Corinthians to encourage them to give to help other poor believers, Paul turns their attention to the Lord Jesus Christ.

He impresses on them, firstly, that the Lord Jesus gave freely: "Ye know the grace of our Lord Jesus Christ". They had come to know this grace in the gospel and it was not a new revelation to them. In return Paul expected them to show grace in their giving to others. There were no 'strings' attached to this act of giving. It was free, without regrets and without ulterior motive. It was all of grace.

Paul also wants them to realise how much the Lord Jesus gave: "Though He was rich yet... He became poor". His riches were those which He enjoyed before He came into this world at Bethlehem. Who can measure them or comprehend them? Yet they were His by right

Realise how much the Lord Jesus gave

and gave Him wealth far beyond your ability to measure. This was what He laid aside when He was born into this world, part of what is involved in Him "emptying Himself" (Phil 2:7). No one ever gave as much as He. No matter what you give it cannot come close to the great sacrifice of the Lord Jesus in leaving the riches of heaven and living in a world where He was despised and rejected.

The great extent of His giving is seen in that He became poor. It would have been an immense downward step from the height of His riches to come into this world as a rich man, but He went further than that. He was born, not into a family wealthy by this world's standards, but into a poor family which enjoyed no position of any importance in the world. Thus He sacrificed what was His by right.

He did it for the blessing and benefit of others

You may ask why He gave so much. It was for the sake of others, that you through His poverty might be made rich. Without selfish motive He did it for the blessing and benefit of others.

He did not give of His possessions, He went beyond that and gave Himself. The expectation of Paul is that your consideration of such an unselfish act for the blessing of others will encourage you to give freely, unselfishly and with the motive of pleasing God and helping others.

Let us do good

"Let us not be weary in well doing . . . let us do good unto all men" (Gal 6:9 -10).

So what then will be your response? Paul exhorts us through the epistle to the Galatians to ensure that we never grow weary in well doing. His desire is that we should never became faint hearted in this work. Over the years we may begin to feel that no real benefit is being derived from our giving and there is little point in continuing. It is true that we may not see the reward for it at the moment, but we are reminded that "in due season we shall reap, if we faint not". We must be constantly looking for opportunities to do good. "As we have therefore opportunity, let us do good", writes the apostle, reminding us that opportunities have to be seized or else they will be lost forever.

Our giving need not be limited to believers, for all men should benefit from what we can give. Care will need to be exercised to ensure that we do not give to what is unworthy of our support, but where real need exists we must endeavour to meet it. This does not encourage us to become wrapped up in the social issues of the day, nor to occupy our time with great social crusades. It does encourage us to be wise and to let it be seen that Christians do have compassionate hearts.

Especially, of course, we are exhorted to remember believers. For example we should be considering constantly the many servants who are labouring in the work of the Lord and who would be helped and encouraged by our gifts, and the many areas of need among Christians which the welfare state does not adequately meet.

Let us, therefore, give the emphasis to this side of christian work which it deserves. May it be said of us that our giving is "an odour of a sweet smell, a sacrifice acceptable, well pleasing to God" (Phil 4:18). Let us remember how sweet is the fragrance in heaven from every gift which is willingly given on earth out of a heart devoted to the Lord Jesus Christ.

Never grow weary in well doing

Let it be seen that Christians do have compassionate hearts